BRITAIN IN OLD PHOTOGRAPHS

CHELMSFORD

JOHN MARRIAGE

High Street, Chelmsford, *c.* 1900.

BRITAIN IN OLD PHOTOGRAPHS

CHELMSFORD

JOHN MARRIAGE

SUTTON PUBLISHING LIMITED

Sutton Publishing Limited
Phoenix Mill · Far Thrupp · Stroud
Gloucestershire · GL5 2BU

First published 1996

Copyright © John Marriage, 1996

British Library Cataloguing in Publication Data
A catalogue record for this book is available from the
British Library.

ISBN 0-7509-0982-X

Typeset in 10/12 Perpetua.
Typesetting and origination by
Sutton Publishing Limited.
Printed in Great Britain by
Ebenezer Baylis, Worcester.

This book is dedicated to the late Miss Hilda Grieves, whose scholarly book, *The Sleepers and the Shadows*, Vols I & II, will always remain the definitive record of Chelmsford's history.

Borough Coat of Arms, 1888 to 1974.

CONTENTS

New Street decorated for Queen Elizabeth II's Coronation in 1953.

INTRODUCTION

Chelmsford, the county town of Essex, is one of the most rapidly growing communities in Europe. It is a pleasant and prosperous modern town within easy commuting distance of London, where many of its inhabitants now work. However, it is also a town of great antiquity though traces of its past are, sadly, rather sparse. Many of the older buildings were ruthlessly swept away earlier this century, some as a result of wartime action but mostly by insensitive developers and bad planning decisions.

The Romans, during their occupation of Britain, built many military roads. One important road ran from London to Colchester and Norwich. Various settlements grew up alongside, including one in the Moulsham area, where a substantial community developed. However, the site of the present town centre remained just a marshy tract of uninhabited land between two rivers. Most scholars agree that the Moulsham settlement was known as *Caesaromagus* (Caesar's field). It is thought to have been abandoned when the Romans left in the fourth century. After their departure the road fell into disuse, probably hastened by the collapse of bridges over the two rivers. The Saxons were the next to settle in Essex. They had little need for roads, but the limited movement they generated passed instead through Writtle, which developed as an important market town. It had the advantage of an easier crossing of the River Can.

The present history of Chelmsford really began in about 1100 when Bishop Maurice bridged the River Can, thereby restoring the original Roman route. In 1199 King John granted permission for a market to be laid out on the triangular piece of land between the River Can and the River Chelmer on the site of the present High Street. Plots of regular dimensions were created around a central market trading area, with each plot running down to the rivers at the rear. A trading community quickly developed offering services to travellers to and from Colchester and Norwich. On the London side the little community was soon to merge with lineal Moulsham village. Writtle's standing was soon eroded by the small town, and its market died.

Geologically, Chelmsford is at the meeting point of Boulder Clay reaching down from North Essex with London Clay stretching up from the Thames estuary. Nearby at Danbury and elsewhere are Bagshot Sands outcrops. These varied soils resulted in favourable conditions for different forms of agriculture with Chelmsford as a natural trading place. In addition, the plentiful supply of flowing water made it a suitable site for the establishment of various industries, such as flour milling, brewing and tanneries, all of which rely heavily on water. With its location in the middle of the county, astride the Great Essex Road, with roads fanning out in all directions, at an early date it became a centre for County administration. By the eighteenth century it was an important stop for scheduled mail and stage coach services, operating from London through to Norwich, Harwich, Sudbury and Bury St Edmunds. The many inns offered food and overnight hospitality to the travellers as well as a change of horses. In turn these activities attracted to the town wheelwrights, saddlers, blacksmiths, horse doctors and others.

Further advances took place in 1797 when the River Chelmer was canalised between the town and the port of Maldon. This made transportation of bulk goods – particularly coal – easier and led to the establishment of more industries, including that of the first inland gas works in the country providing lighting and heating. In the 1840s the railway was built between London, Colchester and Norwich giving even better communications. This, together with the freeing of the Mildmay entail, encouraged further development in the New London Road area and resulted in the establishment of engineering firms like Crompton's, electrical engineers, Hoffmanns, ball-bearing manufacturers and Marconi, electronics. At the turn of the twentieth century they were all growth industries of considerable national significance requiring hundreds of skilled and semi-skilled workers. Consequently, more people were drawn from the surrounding areas and from even further afield. Also in the town were other substantial firms, such as Clarkson Ltd, manufacturers of steam-powered buses that were exported throughout the world. The company Clarkson founded – Eastern National – still has its headquarters in the town, though it is now merely a bus service company. There were also Colman and Morton, agricultural machinery specialists, Eddington & Stevenson, manufacturers of traction engines and Christy and Norris, general engineers. The latter started as a firm specialising in the repair and manufacture of water and wind mills. Today, the town is of far less eminence industrially, though GEC-Marconi has grown into a vast electronic industry and Britvic, from tiny beginnings behind a chemist shop near the cathedral, has become part of an international soft drink industry. Nevertheless, the town remains an important administrative centre for both local and national government offices, including the County Police Authority headquarters. It has several National Health and private hospitals, and many commercial offices are now established there.

In 1888 the town received a Royal Charter making it a municipal borough. Its first mayor was Frederic Chancellor, a local architect and businessman. The borough boundaries were those of the preceding civil parish, which by then had totally absorbed the formerly separate village of Moulsham. At its own request, Springfield, a strongly developing community on the north-east side of the river, remained outside its boundaries, as did the smaller village of Widford.

The next fifty years or so saw various boundary changes which nibbled away at Springfield, and much of the parish was gradually incorporated into the borough. Also absorbed was Widford, together with outlying parts of Broomfield and Writtle. This was in official recognition of the steady outward expansion of the built-up area. By the 1920s the whole of Springfield had become an integral part of the town. Surrounding villages like Great Baddow, Galleywood, Broomfield and Writtle were expanding, and by the 1960s had effectively become detached suburbs of the town. In acceptance of this, when local authority boundaries were changed throughout England and Wales in 1974, Chelmsford Borough and the surrounding Rural District were amalgamated to become a single administrative district. For a time the new authority lost its hard won status as a borough, but this has now been restored. Sadly, even though it has some of the trappings of a city, such as its status as a county and university town, together with being a diocesan seat, complete with a cathedral, its ambition to become a city has so far been denied. Perhaps the forthcoming 900th anniversary of its founding, in 1999, will be an appropriate time for this to be granted.

23/2/96 JM

SECTION ONE

THE TOWN CENTRE

High Street, *c*. 1900. Its important junction with Springfield Road was marked by a graceful rotunda, popularly known as 'The Conduit'. It was originally in Tindal Square, but was replaced by the present Judge Tindal statue. 'The Conduit' is now in Tower Gardens.

Tindal Square was an important meeting point for townspeople on occasions ranging from the weekly market to celebrations of national and local events. As a result of changes in the 1960s, it is now little more than an awkwardly shaped road junction.

High Street. In the late nineteenth century, many of the properties were still in private hands. Mounted on a granite plinth in front of the Shire Hall was the imposing Sebastopol Cannon, now banished to Oaklands Park.

Tindal Street from the cathedral tower, c. 1910. Visually this was one of the most attractive streets in the town until one side was removed in the 1960s to make way for the present efficient, but architecturally dull, High Chelmer shopping precinct.

Duke Street, seen from Tindal Square looking towards the railway station, *c.* 1900. At its entrance was the curiously bowed Golden Lion public house, now replaced by a 1960s office block.

In 1900 New London Road, from the Iron Bridge to High Street, was flanked on one side by Museum Terrace, a substantial block of early Victorian properties, and on the other by Wenley's gardens and stables.

This sketch, dating from the 1940s, shows the junction of High Street and New London Road. The old timber-framed shops were demolished to allow road widening shortly afterwards.

Duke Street, *c*. 1910. The present substantial white stone-faced County Hall replaced many of the buildings on the right about twenty-five years later.

Chelmsford Cathedral was masked from Duke Street by this group of small properties, *c*. 1910.

SHIRE HALL, CHELMSFORD.

The Shire Hall is unquestionably Chelmsford's most distinguished public building. It was built in 1792 by John Johnson, then Surveyor to the county, and commands a dominating position at the head of the High Street.

The entrance to Market Road from Tindal
Square, with a glimpse of the Golden Lion and
County Hall in the distance, *c.* 1945.

New Street, *c.* 1900. Until postwar times the police station stood almost opposite the side of the Shire
Hall, with the adjoining terrace mainly in residential use. A tunnel is reputed to have existed between the
station and the Shire Hall, to enable prisoners to be moved easily from the police cells to the courts.
Today, although the old station still survives, a much larger police station has been built further down the
road, displacing houses and small shops.

Until the construction of The Parkway in the 1960s the New London Road junction with High Street was always very busy, requiring the services of a policeman on point duty.

High Street, *c.* 1955. In those days it was still possible to park a car outside the shop of one's choice and to make a leisurely purchase, without incurring the wrath of a traffic warden.

This sketch, dating from about 1850, depicts the site of The Meadows. In those times the marshy land was used merely for grazing. In the distance is the Horsepond Bridge.

In about 1910 Moulsham Street was a very picturesque part of the town. Sadly, in the 1960s The Parkway sliced through at this point, leaving the upper street somewhat isolated from the town centre.

Moulsham Street towards High Street, *c*. 1910. In the distance and on the far side of Moulsham Bridge is the old Methodist Church (see also page 84). It was replaced in the 1960s with possibly the ugliest high-rise office block in the area.

The Methodist Church was built in Victorian times beside the River Can, on the site of an earlier public house. In turn, it was superseded by the Cater building.

This fascinating early aerial photograph of about 1920 shows the town spreading out from the Shire Hall and the cathedral. The open countryside in the distance is now mostly developed.

The lower part of High Street and The Conduit, *c.* 1900. Nearby was the Kings Head Hotel, once one of the most attractive inns in the town. Demolished in the 1920s, it was replaced by Woolworth's 3*d* and 6*d* store.

Duke Street, *c*. 1920. Although many of the buildings remain they have since been converted from the small shops and houses shown here to substantial businesses.

The Eastern National Bus Company's garage in Duke Street, *c*. 1930. Subsequently the company acquired additional land, and in the late 1930s built the present station.

ENVIRONS

Two views of the upper end of Moulsham Street, *c.* 1910. Many of the buildings remain but the sleepy appearance has gone for ever.

In about 1905 Rainsford Road was a quiet residential road leading towards Bishops Stortford and Hertford.

Maltese Road was built in late Victorian times with spacious houses for prosperous middle-class townspeople.

Old Court Road is a short cul-de-sac off Springfield Road built in the 1920s. It provides typical artisan accommodation of the times.

Springfield Place is a beautiful Georgian mansion next to the church. For several years it was the home of John Strutt (1727–1827), the owner of Springfield and Moulsham mills. He later built, and moved to, Terling Place.

Lawn Lane, Springfield, *c.* 1930. Until postwar years it was a quiet country lane.

Arbour Lane, Springfield, at the turn of the century. It is reputed that the terrace houses were built to house railway construction workers.

In 1900 Widford was a separate village on the fringe of Chelmsford. Its single street has since been absorbed almost without trace into the town.

The centre portion of Hylands House was built in 1730 by Sir John Comyns. During the nineteenth century a portico and two wings were added. In Victorian times there were further extensions, but these were removed by Chelmsford Borough Council, the current owner, thereby restoring its nineteenth-century appearance.

For many years Hylands House was the family residence of the Hanbury family. One of the attractions was a large indoor swimming pool, converted from a greenhouse. It was demolished in 1966.

The interior of the greenhouse when it was still filled with many exotic plants.

Early this century Writtle was a self-contained village. For many people the sole link with Chelmsford was a Great Eastern Railway bus, which ran a shuttle service to and from the railway station.

At the turn of the century Great Baddow was a large village, which had grown up around the junction of Southend Road with the Maldon road. Nevertheless, in about 1905 it had a very quiet and rural appearance.

As Chelmsford expands, many hectares of prime agricultural land disappear under bricks and mortar. Here land is being harrowed at Nabbotts Farm in 1950. Most of the farm has since been developed.

In 1950 Nabbotts Farm still made considerable use of horses and carts.

SHOPS AND SHOPPING

Clarke's the bookshop has provided generations of Chelmsfordians with a first-class book and stationery service. Part of the extensive first floor bookshop is shown here. On the right Miss Clarke – no relation to the owners – attends a customer.

The exterior of J.H. Clarke & Co's premises, *c.* 1950. Until relocation in the 1960s, they had an island site midway down High Street. The premises are now occupied by Lloyds Bank.

Clarke's provided a personal service, with an extensive range of drawing office and general office materials in a relatively small area on the ground floor at their High Street premises. It is seen here in about 1950.

Local activities were always enthusiastically supported by tradespeople. Here, Bolingbroke and Sons have lavishly decorated their High Street shop to celebrate an agricultural event held in the town, *c.* 1900.

WHERE TO SHOP AT CHELMSFORD.

Telegrams :
" Bolingbrokes,
Chelmsford."

Telephone :
0193, Chelmsford.

G. J. Bolingbroke & Sons,

COSTUMIERS & LADIES' TAILORS,
— HIGH-CLASS —

MILLINERS & LADIES' OUTFITTERS,

General Drapers & Linen Merchants.

G. J. B. & SONS hold a First-class Diploma for

...LADIES' TAILORING.

Perfect Fit and Style Guaranteed.

G. J. B. & SONS have the largest High-class

DRESSMAKING DEPARTMENT
in the district.

SPECIALISTS IN FURWORK.

MOURNING ORDERS SPECIALLY CATERED FOR.

FUNERALS COMPLETELY FURNISHED,
and Personally Conducted in all parts of the country.

AGENTS { BURBERRY'S RAINPROOF CLOTHING.
FOR   { PULLAR DYE WORKS, PERTH.

ESTIMATES GIVEN, AND CATALOGUES ON APPLICATION.

74 & 75, High Street, Chelmsford.

Bolingbroke and Sons offered an extensive Ladies outfitting service in about 1910, as this advertisement shows.

In postwar years Bolingbroke's established a children's department in New London Road, opposite their main shop. It was swept away when the High Chelmer precinct was built in the 1960s.

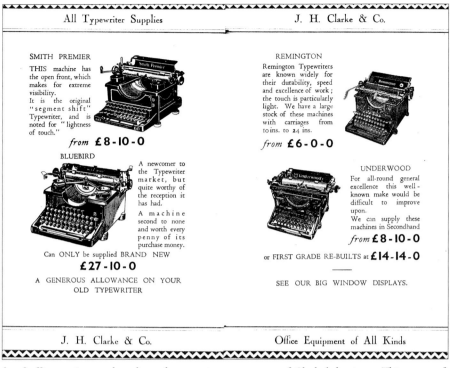

The sale of office equipment has always been an important part of Clarke's business. This extract from a sales brochure of about 1950 shows a selection of some of their latest typewriters.

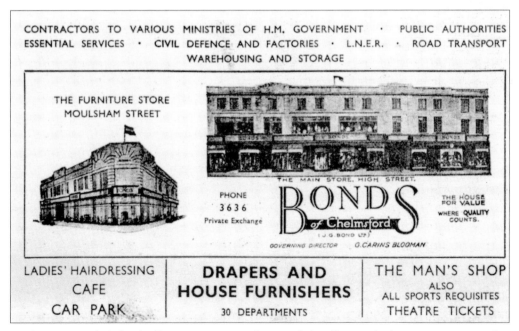

Bonds was one of Chelmsford's most important shops, and this illustrated advertisement appeared in about 1944. Sadly, in postwar years this locally owned business was taken over by Debenhams, who have since considerably expanded its floor space.

The Golden Fleece in Duke Street was one of the town's most popular hotels, and in the 1950s its first floor restaurant was a popular dining room. It has now been rather absurdly renamed the Rat & Parrot, severing a link with the town's past as a market and wool trading centre.

At the entrance to New Street and outwardly still unchanged are these two substantial buildings. Nearest is the Neo-Georgian Barclays Bank, built in 1905 from a design by Sir Reginald Blomfield. Although much altered internally it is still occupied by the same bank. Next door is the former General Post Office, built almost concurrently, to house the post office, sorting and telephone exchange. All these services now occupy separate buildings elsewhere.

Chelmsford's livestock market was originally in the High Street and Tindal Square but was moved in 1880 to purpose-made premises on the south side of Market Road. It has since gone to Springfield, and the Market Road site is now a multi-storey car park.

Opposite the livestock market was a substantial poultry market together with agricultural machinery showrooms. County Hall has now been extended to occupy the land.

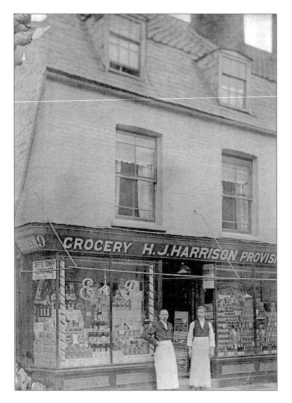

H.J. Harrison, long-established family grocers, had premises in Duke Street, close to the cathedral. The shop closed in the 1960s.

Chelmsford boasted several temperance hotels in about 1900. The Red Cow, at the corner of Broomfield Road and Rainsford Road, was one of the largest. The owner, Mr Bausor, stands proudly at the entrance gate. The building remains, but its pleasant setting has disappeared.

Wenley & Son, seen here in about 1900, was the town's largest furniture shop. Their bedroom furniture gallery is illustrated.

It was Wenley & Son's policy to encourage customers to browse. They were able to offer a wide selection of heavily ornate dining and sitting room furniture of the period.

WORK

Marconi established his first factory in Chelmsford in 1898. Since then the firm has played an important role in the industrial life of the town. The front of their factory in New Street is shown here, *c.* 1920.

Mast riggers, 1920.

In the early 1920s Marconi erected several huge masts in connection with his research. These towered above the town, and were demolished just before the last war. At the base of one are a group of riggers.

In 1912 Marconi's main factory in New Street was built in the record time of seventeen weeks. Some of the 500 building workers employed stand in tiered ranks on the scaffolding.

The Hoffman Manufacturing Company was established in New Street at the turn of the century, principally to make ball bearings. The first building was a long single-storey structure set at right angles to the road. The picture shows part of the complex in the 1930s.

Hoffmann's main drawing office, c. 1950.

In their heyday Hoffmann's produced a huge range of ball bearings and their races. Here, a First World War worker demonstrates one of the largest ever produced.

Hoffmann's grinding shop, c. 1915. Each machine was powered via belt drive from overhead shafts. The company had its own power supply.

Most able-bodied men were called into the Armed Forces during the First World War. This resulted in the first recruitment ever of female labour. The somewhat dirty work at Hoffmann's necessitated heavy overalls and, for safety reasons, hair was completely enclosed in a snood.

Next to Hoffmann's and Marconi's were several other industries, including a large maltsters. The town's railway goods yard was also close by.

Springfield Mill, seen here in about 1900, had a chequered career like many water mills. In addition to flour grinding it also undertook chemical processing. A steam engine was housed in the small brick building to augment the water wheels. The latter was removed in 1926 to allow Victoria Road to be constructed.

Col. R.E. Crompton (1845–1940) examines the original alternator at Chelmsford Power Station in Anchor Street, before it was dismantled between the wars, when the town was connected to the national grid.

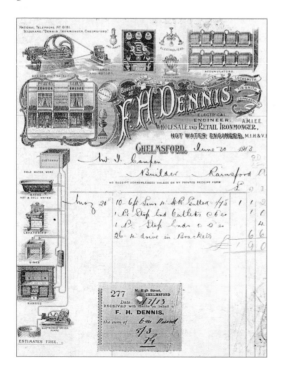

This ornate Victorian letterhead includes among its illustrations the text book way of installing a hot and cold water supply system.

Before the construction of High Chelmer, J.H. Clarke & Co. printed many of the local traders' posters and booklets at their works in Union Yard, off Tindal Street. One of their printing machines is seen in action.

Messrs J. Campen were long-established jobbing builders with premises in Rainsford Road. In the lower picture Mr Campen poses with two of his employees.

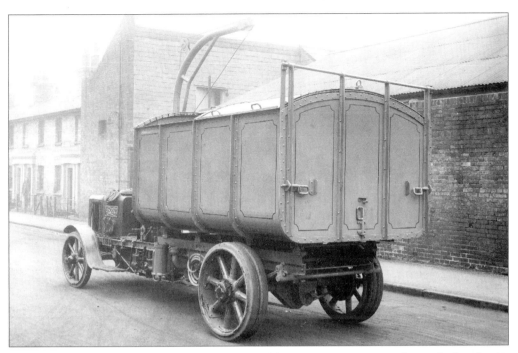

This steam-driven refuse vehicle, made by the National Steam Car Company, stands outside their factory in Queens Street, *c.* 1916. Although the company's buses were, for a time, a considerable commercial success, few refuse vehicles were sold.

At the turn of the century Munnion & Sons had a substantial coach and carriage business in Springfield Road. Initially they specialised in making horse-drawn carriages, but later produced the bodywork for most of Clarkson's steam buses and for early car manufacturers. The site has now been redeveloped as part of The Meadows shopping centre.

This 'Chelmsford' steam bus was built at Clarkson's Moulsham Street works, with coachwork added by Munnion & Sons. It was one of two sold to the North Eastern Railway Company in 1905.

The interior of a 'Chelmsford' steam bus. They were built to provide a high standard of comfort, and were reputed to be quiet – and warm in winter.

TRANSPORT

This sketch shows part of the southern side of Springfield Navigation Basin, *c.* 1910. The nearest barge, 'Seven Brothers', was owned by May & Butcher of Heybridge Basin and brought coal and other materials to Chelmsford.

Right from the opening of the navigation in 1797, timber was shipped up to Coates Wharf at Springfield Basin. The extensive timber warehouses of Brown & Sons are shown here in about 1930.

The 14 mile Chelmer & Blackwater Navigation passes through delightful rural countryside between Chelmsford and Heybridge Basin. Pictured here in about 1910 is a maintenance barge carrying downstream a new lock gate for one of the thirteen locks.

Wenley's ran a removal service for many years. At first their vehicles were horsedrawn and travel was slow and laborious. Later they acquired steam vehicles before turning to motor lorries.

Chelmsford from Arbour Lane bridge, showing the Great Eastern Railway line to the station, *c.* 1920. Beside is Bunny Walk, a popular lovers' lane. In those days the track passed through open fields almost to the town centre.

Chelmsford railway station, *c*. 1905. Two cumbersome Great Eastern Railway Stratford-built petrol buses stand on the forecourt. The appearance of the station remained unchanged until it was totally rebuilt in the 1980s.

A Great Eastern train pulls away from Chelmsford station, *c*. 1905.

The staff of J.H. Clarke & Co. posed for this group picture during their annual coach trip, 1929.

This National Bus Company charabanc was photographed in Moulsham Street just before a day's outing to the coast, *c.* 1920.

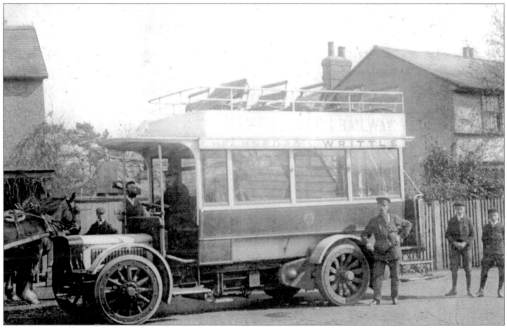

The Great Eastern Railway operated their petrol-driven buses in the Chelmsford area from 1905 until they were withdrawn in 1914. They were replaced by National steamers.

In 1910 motor vehicles were still rare and the Tuffnell family at Langleys owned one of the first in the Chelmsford area. Their smartly dressed chauffeur in his warm uniform is pictured standing proudly beside the motor.

Thomas Clarkson (standing on the right), managing director of the National Steam Car Company, together with some of his drivers and conductresses in Viaduct Road, *c.* 1915. The buses were parked overnight in one of the arches.

Hoffmann munition workers about to leave Chelmsford railway station for a day outing in August 1916 to Clacton-on-Sea, using National steam buses.

Brown & Sons had steam-driven vehicles in the 1920s and '30s before transferring to petrol and diesel. The company took delivery of this 'Sentinel' lorry in 1934.

An Eastern National bus on a scheduled service from West Avenue to Finchley Avenue passing along Duke Street, c. 1950.

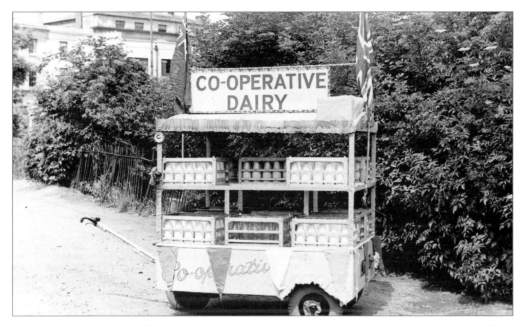

In early postwar years the Chelmsford Co-operative Society operated these power assisted hand vehicles throughout the built-up areas of the town.

Motor scooters were very popular and stylish during the 1950s, providing a very easy form of transport in relative comfort. Here, Miss Peggy Arnett of Hill House, Broomfield displays her 125 cc Douglas Vespa.

In the 1950s, Hoffmann's were still employing huge numbers of workers at their New Street plant. As a result there was massive traffic congestion when the shifts changed.

An Eastern National bus passing the station forecourt, 1950s. In those days the driver was totally segregated from passengers in his own cabin. The conductor was in charge and collected the fares.

SECTION SIX

WATERWAYS

A short section of the River Can next to Admirals Park has been a popular paddling place for generations of young children. This was a summer scene in the 1930s.

For years this curved ironwork bridge provided access to the Chelmsford City Football Club from the Recreation Ground (now Central Park). In the 1980s it was replaced after some years of dereliction.

A stroll beside the River Can in the Recreation Ground has always been popular. These walkers are passing the site of the present Parkway bridge, *c.* 1920.

The Bell Meadow, *c.* 1910. A children's play area now occupies the site.

Moulsham Bridge is one of the few unchanging features of the town. This elegant structure was built in 1787 from a design by John Johnson. Its single span is surmounted by sturdy balusters, made from Coade stone.

Another attractive crossing of the River Can is the New London Road bridge, built towards the end of last century. This picture shows it framed by greenery. Since the 1960s, however, its appearance has been abused by the replacement of the natural banks by sheer concrete walls.

The River Chelmer near Victoria Road, *c*. 1920. In those days it was framed by pastureland. In the far distance there is a glimpse of the town centre. A retail park was constructed in the 1980s on the far side of the river.

The River Chelmer looking upstream from Victoria Road, *c.* 1910. There was a small dairy on the left bank with water meadows opposite.

Before the flood prevention scheme of the 1960s, the River Chelmer had several small alternative channels. One of these led under Horsepond bridge into the Horsepond before rejoining the main course. This rare photograph of about 1950 is one of the few pictures taken showing the medieval arches of the bridge, which were demolished when the Horsepond was filled in.

Before the flood prevention scheme was carried out, the River Chelmer and the River Can united at Moulsham Mill. However, a minor channel known as 'The Gullet', seen here in about 1950, ran along the rear of shops in High Street, and also connected the two rivers. Sadly, this potentially attractive feature of the town was infilled in the 1960s.

Enthusiasts from the Inland Waterways Association had a day's barge trip from Chelmsford to Heybridge Basin in 1955 (see also page 112). Fred Hoy leads the famous barge horse Chelmsford Duke.

When first held in about 1955, the annual Chelmsford to Heybridge Basin canoe race was started from beneath the Chelmer Road bridge.

Barnes Mill, Springfield, *c.* 1920. In postwar years it ceased to be a working mill, and has now been converted into a house with offices.

Another view of Barnes Mill. In the late 1940s a large sea scout unit was based in the grounds. They erected a nissen hut beside the mill stream where their boats were moored.

Rivers in Chelmsford are normally very placid. Nevertheless, when in spate they can become swift flowing and a challenge for experienced paddlers. Here, in about 1955, two canoeists are seen 'shooting' a weir near Broomfield.

SERVICES

The Cathedral Church of St Mary seen from the air, *c.* 1925. It was originally the parish church for the town, but was elevated to cathedral status in 1913 when the Anglican Diocese of Chelmsford was created.

The Congregational Church, built in 1840, was in New London Road. Its exterior was made of Mildmay bricks, five bays wide with a three bay pediment and a loggia of four Greek columns at ground floor. It was demolished in the 1960s and the site is now occupied by a furniture store.

St Mary's interior as it appeared in the last century. The nave has recently been remodelled and the fixed pews swept away.

CHELMSFORD, WESLEYAN CHURCH

The High Street Methodist Church was built in 1898 on the site of a former public house. It had room for 500 worshippers on two floors and there was a school at the rear. It was demolished in the 1960s to make way for the present incredibly ugly office block.

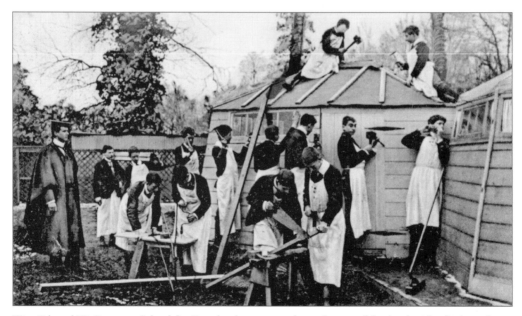

King Edward VI Grammar School for Boys has been a popular and successful school with a high academic record for all of its long history. Here, in about 1900, under the watchful eye of a master, pupils are assembling a small nursing hospital tent.

A classroom scene at the King Edward VI Grammar School, *c.* 1905.

Pupils from the King Edward VI Grammar School, *c.* 1950.

Chelmsford County High School for Girls has an excellent academic record and currently ranks as one of the best in the whole country.

This brick and stone building in Victoria Road South, photographed in about 1930, is now part of Anglia University. It was built in 1905, with a library and museum on the ground floor and a school of art and technology on the upper floor.

Hoffmann's maintained their own fire brigade for many years. The First World War brigade is shown here, together with various items of equipment. The off-duty hat in those days followed the style of a sailor's cap.

The Essex County Police Force was established in 1840 and moved to its present headquarters at New Court in Springfield in 1903, about the time this group picture was taken.

Old Court, Springfield, *c.* 1890, when it was the County Police Headquarters. Before their occupation it was a military depot. It has recently been converted into housing.

The Drill Hall in Market Road (now Victoria Road South) was built for the Chelmsford Volunteers in 1903 and opened by Field Marshal Lord Roberts VC and Field Marshal Sir Evelyn Wood VC. It was demolished in 1995.

Essex County Council built Broomfield Sanatorium in the grounds of Broomfield Court in the late 1930s for the treatment of tuberculosis. It is now a general NHS hospital, and there have since been major alterations and extensions.

The original entrance to the County Police Headquarters from New Court Road, *c.* 1925. Although structurally unchanged, the entrance is now sealed.

The County Police Headquarters was built in 1903 in the form of a crescent grouped around a green area. These buildings remain substantially unchanged, although at the rear major extensions have been built.

The matron at Chelmsford and Essex Hospital poses for this group picture, together with doctors and nurses, *c*. 1930.

A prison has existed in the town since the seventeenth century. The present gaol at Springfield was opened in 1828 and the exterior has remained substantially unchanged. Subsequently land in the foreground has been built on.

Chelmsford has always been a fairly law abiding town; nevertheless, there were frequent cases of petty crime. In about 1940 local detectives took time off to pose for this group picture.

LEISURE

The interior of the Regent Theatre, built 1916, was highly decorated. The upstairs foyer, now a mere alcove next to the stairs, was in Palm Court style.

The exterior of the Regent Theatre soon after it opened in 1913. At first it was used solely for stage productions, but with the coming of talkies it became mainly a cinema. It is now a bingo hall.

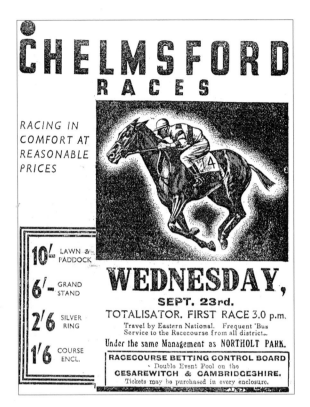

Horse racing was held at Galleywood from 1759 and ended in the late 1930s. The course, completely encircling the church, is unique. This advertisement appeared in the local press in September 1936.

For four days, commencing Boxing Day 1928, the Regent Theatre staged the musical comedy 'So this is Love'. It had a large cast, and played to packed houses.

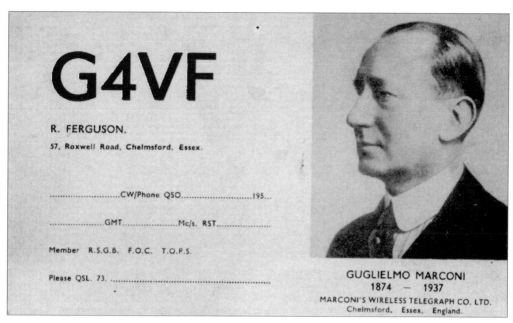

Chelmsford played a unique role in the birth of radio so it is not surprising that a substantial number of radio hams lived in the area. In the late 1940s one such enthusiast was Ronald Ferguson of Roxwell Road, whose call sign was G4VF.

In 1958 Writtle School were the champions of Division II of Chelmsford Schools Football League. This group picture of the team, together with their teachers, was taken on Writtle Green.

THREE FEET DEEP

The town's first swimming pool was opened in 1906 in Waterloo Lane, with a clay floor that was fairly quickly replaced by concrete. This picture was taken in the late 1940s when it reopened following war damage.

The Corn Exchange dominated Tindal Square from 1857 until its demolition in the 1960s. Throughout its existence it was available for a multitude of public activities from dancing to exhibitions.

Before the days of mass commercial entertainment, summer garden parties were eagerly awaited events. This group picture was taken at Springfield Hill in about 1900.

The Chelmsford Horse Show, traditionally held in Kings Head Meadow was an annual event well into postwar years. Here, Fred Hoy receives the prize for the best turned-out horse and cart.

The Essex Hunt meet in front of Hylands House at the turn of the century. As the estate comprised 440 acres there was plenty of scope to enjoy the chase.

Members and supporters of the Chelmsford Athletic Club gather to record the initial run of this now long-established Club.

EVENTS

Even now, hidden behind the façades of some High Street properties, ancient timber-framed structures remain and, unfortunately, still present a fire hazard. In 1947 the west side of High Street was threatened by a serious outbreak at Wenley's and Bolingbroke's, then independent shops. Luckily the fire brigade was able to contain the blaze, but both shops were completely gutted – as these two photographs show.

Chelmsford Carnival Procession has always been a popular annual event, with hundreds of spectators lining the route. Here, John Bull and a military band lead the procession from New London Road into High Street, *c.* 1935.

In the 1950 Carnival procession, members of the Chelmsford Boating (now Canoe) Club paraded their canoe 'Chelmer Queen' round the streets.

Floats decorated as boats have always been firm favourites in the procession. A particularly skilful one, built around a milk float, appeared in the 1938 event.

In about 1915 the funeral procession of Col. Fred Taylor, founder of the present firm of estate agents, was a sombre military affair with a substantial cortège and many bystanders.

The removal of The Conduit from the junction of High Street and Springfield Road, in about 1938, was a sad day, denying the town of its most attractive piece of street furniture. Sadly, a recent opportunity for it to be returned has been missed.

A procession marking Co-operators' Day brought together a substantial number of milk floats, bakers' roundsmen and butchers' carts, in an impressive parade, *c*. 1930.

A tour of the town centre for the annual Co-operators' Day procession ended at the Co-operative Society offices. Here, a column of children in fancy dress turn into Barrack Street, *c*. 1930.

In 1927 Father Christmas arrived at Chelmsford by biplane. His destination was Bolingbroke's shop in High Street.

In July 1888 there was a serious summer flood and most of the properties in the centre were inundated, causing an immense amount of damage. This was the scene in Springfield Road.

In 1958 there was another summer flood, with similar disruption and damage to the whole of the town centre. A flood prevention scheme was subsequently instituted.

Each year the Directors of the Chelmer & Blackwater Navigation inspect their waterway by boat. In 1955 they used a converted barge. It was pulled by Chelmsford Duke, who was led by Fred Hoy, and is shown here passing Barnes Mill.

This Georgian town house in High Street was patriotically decorated for Queen Victoria's Golden Jubilee in 1887. In 1905 the house was replaced by the present Barclays Bank.

WARTIME

Substantial numbers of troops were stationed in and around Chelmsford during the First World War. They were part of the strategic reserve, held throughout East Anglia in case of invasion. In about 1915 a column of soldiers was pictured marching through Tindal Square.

Lord Kitchener inspecting soldiers of the Royal Artillery at Hylands Park, *c.* 1914.

In 1915 a book sale was held at J.H. Clarke's shop in High Street to raise funds for the British Red Cross.

Chelmsford's factories were engaged in military work during both world wars. At Hoffmann's women turned out munitions, which was heavy and dirty work. In 1915 these girls were photographed wearing the clean overalls they started their shift in.

During the Second World War many shops partially covered their plate glass windows as a protection against shards of flying glass. In 1944 H.J. Harrison, whose shop was in Duke Street, commissioned this picture, recording a typical wartime display.

RUNNING WITHOUT PETROL

A considerable number of 'Buses have been adapted by the Company to run on PRODUCER GAS

★ALREADY THE "EASTERN NATIONAL" AND THE COMPANIES ASSOCIATED WITH IT, HAVE RUN 2,500,000 MILES BY THIS MEANS, SAVING 415,000 GALLONS OF IMPORTED FUEL

Throughout the Second World War there was a severe shortage of petrol, and various ingenious solutions were forthcoming. The Eastern National converted some of their buses to run on gas.

Chelmsford suffered intense raids on 15 April and 14 May 1943, and there was considerable damage each time. This was the scene at the Police Headquarters after the second raid.

As part of Chelmsford's air defences a battery of rocket launchers were installed in the Recreation Ground (now Central Park) together with ammunition dumps and shelters. They were manned by the Home Guard, who claimed several hits.

Bofors Light Anti-Aircraft guns were installed in various places around the town, including on the roof of Marconi's factory. Here, a group of Home Guard gunners are pictured in front of a Bofors with some of its ammunition.

Air raid shelters were installed in many places. The Government supplied many houses with Anderson or Morrison shelters. Some, however, were erected privately, as was this surface shelter in Victoria Road.

The first plane to be brought down in Chelmsford during the Battle of Britain in 1940 was a Heinkel. It fell in Bishops Court, Springfield Road.

With civilian clothing severely rationed, many shops had to rely on the sale of officers' and other ranks' uniforms to keep the tills ringing.

PEOPLE

David Smith, the well-known local author, with his
mother, Margaret and cousin, Miss Peggy Arnett, at Hill
House, Broomfield, *c*. 1950.

Springfield Scouts make ready for camp, possibly at Danbury, *c*. 1930.

Mrs Mary Ann Chittock, with her dog Rover, at Great Sir Hughs Farm, Great Baddow, *c.* 1900. Her husband was farm bailiff.

Mrs Sarah Clarke, the founder of J.H. Clarke and Co., *c.* 1920.

The Chelmsford band of the Salvation Army, photographed at their headquarters at the Citadel in Moulsham Street, 1906.

A 'shoot' gathers at Hill House, Broomfield, for a day's sport in the nearby woods and meadows.

Early this century, a fund-raising bazaar was held by Wesleyan Methodists at the Corn Exchange, when a varied programme of entertainment took place.

The author's father, Harry Marriage (right), with two friends at Cottage Place, 1925. On the left is Richard Spalding, a relative of Fred Spalding, the famous Chelmsford photographer who took many of the pictures that appear in this book.

ACKNOWLEDGEMENTS

The photographs appear by kind permission of the following: Mrs J. Bailey, Bolingbroke & Wenley Ltd, Mr N. Bowdidge, Clarke's of Chelmsford, Mr J. Clements, Chelmsford Star Co-operative Society Ltd, Mrs J. Dunmow, Eastern National Omnibus Co. Ltd, Essex Police Authority, Essex Records Office, Executors of Mrs J. Jackson, Executors of Mr J. Oliver, GEC-Marconi, Mr A. Hoy, Mr and Mrs P.J. James, Loco. Club of Great Britain, Mrs Marshall, Mr V. Marriage, Mrs J. Matthams, Mr S.A. Norton, Mr A. Osborne, Mr E. Pearson, Mrs Sewell, Mr R. Tippler, and Mrs P. Trevor. Others come from the author's own collection.